Not My Car

Written by
Jill Atkins

This car is long.

"That is not my car," my dad tells me.

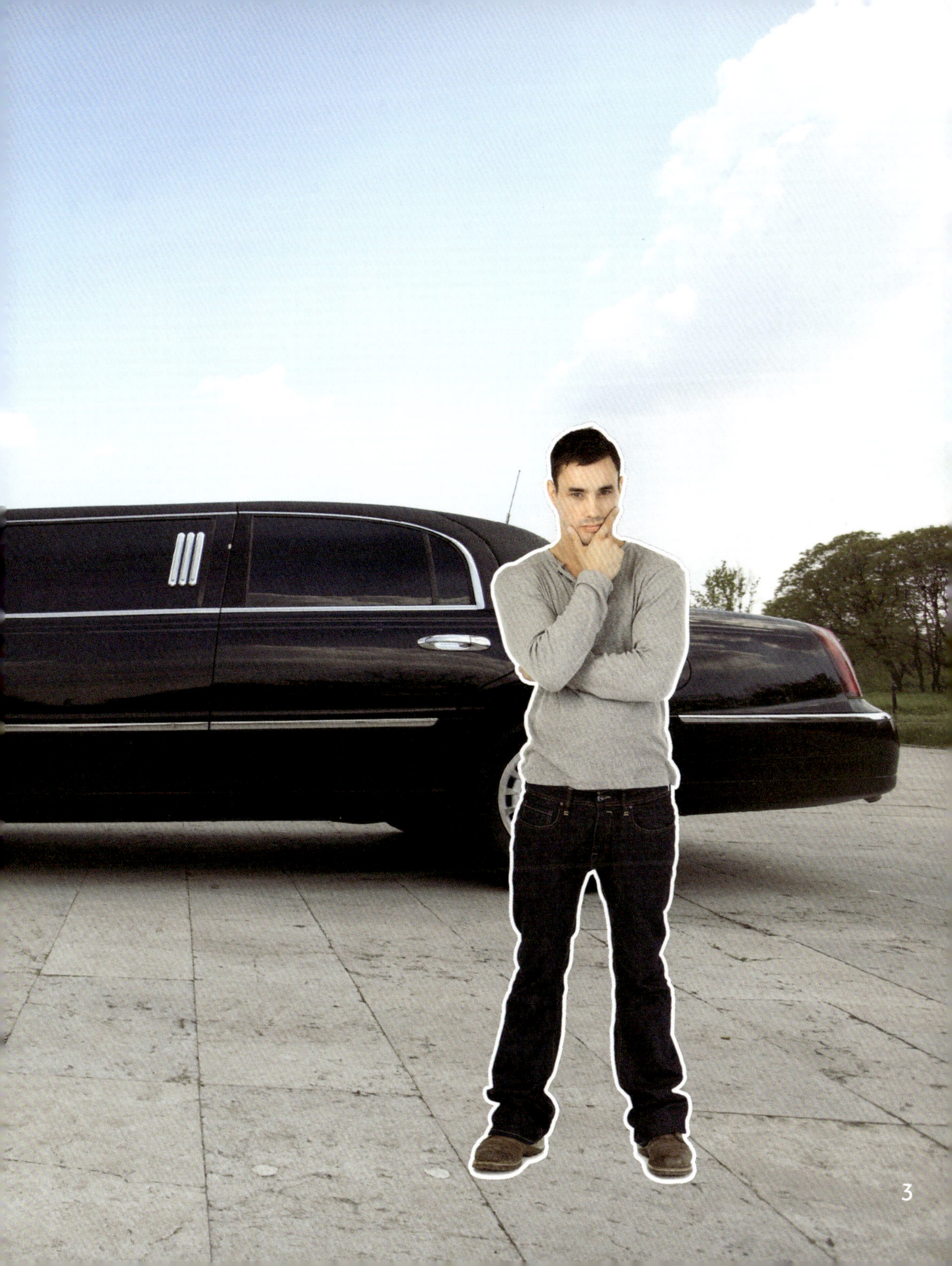

This car is in a big park.

"That is not my car. That is a kids' car," my dad tells me.

This car is in a barn.

"That is not my car.
I can tell," my dad tells me.

This car is in a yard.

"That is not my car!"
my dad tells me in a rush.

This car is at the market.

"Is that my car? No, it is not!" my dad tells me.

This car is in a car park.

"No, that is not my car," my dad tells me.

This car is in the garden.

"Ha! Ha! The car in the garden is not my car," my dad tells me.

This car is on the farm.

"That cannot be my car," my dad tells me. "That car is rubbish!"

This car has far to go.

"That car is quick," my dad tells me. "But it is not my car."

My dad has not got a car.
He has a big van!

Off we go!